CHICKEN KETO RECIPES

50 Easy and Delicious Ketogenic Diet Recipes

By Elaine Chasey

© 2023 Elaine Chasey All Rights Reserved
All rights reserved. No part of this publication may be reproduced, distributed,
or transmitted in any form or by any means, including photocopying, recording,
or other electronic or mechanical methods, without the prior written permission of the publisher,
except in the case of brief quotations embodied in critical reviews
and certain other noncommercial uses permitted by copyright law.

Contents

Introduction 5

Baked Chicken Wings with the Dipping Sauce 8

Baked Chicken with Garlic and Lemons 9

Baked Paprika Chicken Wings with Keto Ketchup 10

Balsamic Cranberry Roast Chicken 11

Buffalo Chicken Celery Sticks 12

Chicken Breasts Stuffed with Antipasti 13

Chicken Breasts Stuffed with Broccoli and Cheese 14

Chicken Breasts Stuffed with Spinach and Feta Cheese 15

Chicken Creamy Broccoli Casserole 16

Chicken Creamy Soup 17

Chicken Drumsticks baked 18

Chicken in Wine (Coq au Vin) 19

Chicken Lettuce Wraps 20

Chicken Meatballs with Flavored Melt Butter inside 21

Chicken Meatballs with Marinara sauce 22

Creamy Chicken with Mushrooms 23

Chicken Pan with Vegetables 24

Chicken Parmesan Casserole with Spaghetti Squash 25

Chicken Parmesan Stuffed Peppers 26

Chicken patties with Bella Mushrooms 27

Chicken Pot Pie 28

Chicken Ranch Casserole 29

Chicken Breasts with Zucchini, Tomatoes, and Mozzarella 30

Chicken Thighs baked in Tomato Sauce 31

Chicken Thighs baked with Eggplant and Cheese 32

Chicken baked with Orange Sweet and Sour Sauce 33

Rotisserie Stuffed Chicken 34

- Chicken with Prunes and Dried Apricots 35
- Chicken Zoodles 36
- Chili Lime Chicken Drumsticks 37
- Cornish Game Hens with Garlic and Rosemary 38
- Creamy Baked Chicken 39
- Zucchini Chicken Rolls 40
- Rotisserie Chicken Spinach Casserole 41
- Crispy Spicy Chicken Wings 42
- Garlic Parmesan Chicken Wings 43
- Italian Chicken Breasts 44
- Jalapeno Pepper Chicken Casserole 45
- Parmesan Chicken Drumsticks 46
- Pesto Chicken Casserole 47
- Pesto Parmesan Chicken 48
- Rotisserie Chicken and Salad Lunch Bowl 49
- Sheet Pan Chicken Sausage and Vegetables 50
- Sheet Pan Chicken with Green Vegetables 51
- Spicy Chicken Drumsticks 52
- Teriyaki Chicken Drumsticks 53
- Tex Mex Chicken Salad 54
- Zucchini and Ground Chicken Boats 55
- Zucchini Chicken Lasagna 56
- Buffalo Chicken Wings 57
- Best Foods to eat on the Keto Diet 58

INTRODUCTION

Have you decided recently to change your diet and go keto? Then you are probably looking for new and healthy ways to cook your favorite dishes.

Most ketogenic diet plans recommend you stay between 15 - 30g of net carbohydrates per day, making 5-10% of total calories. But if you're a very active person and exercise 4 to 5 times a week, you can consume more carbohydrates. But remember that you shouldn't have a meat dish at every meal.

So, you are probably wondering what can be a good substitute for the majority of your meals. Non-starchy veggies like spinach and kale, avocado, bell peppers, and tomatoes are great for keto.

Some dairy products are excellent protein, fat, potassium, and calcium sources. You may use butter, hard and soft cheeses, whipping cream, cottage cheese, sour cream, and plain yogurt for cooking keto meals. But make sure that dairy products containing large quantities of sugar should be eliminated from your diet (ice cream, flavored kinds of milk, sweetened yogurts).

Chicken meat is one of the essential products in western cuisine. And chicken dishes are widely popular in many countries of the world. You can make a nutritious lunch meal, a delicious, elegant dinner course, a tasty breakfast, or finger food with chicken.

With zero carbs, chicken is keto-approved. Try to choose dark meat for more fat and iron. Remember that high-protein foods have a very low content of fiber, which may cause constipation. So, make sure to add fiber to your chicken like spinach, kale, carrots, tomatoes, asparagus, and zucchini.

There are so many ways to cook chicken. Picante spices and herbs will add extraordinary flavor to your dishes. And creative combinations of vegetables, cooking oils, cheese, and all kinds of condiments will blow your taste buds away.

Remember that the keto diet, like any other type of diet, is a very individual way to eat. And you must always talk to your doctor to make sure that you choose the right food products to help you become healthier.

So put on your apron and get ready to cook like a chef!

> Nutrition facts are provided as a courtesy using the WPRM recipe calculator. It is best to make your calculations to ensure accuracy. We expressly disclaim any liability concerning any act or omission wholly or in part in reliance on anything contained in this book. Percent Daily Values are based on a 2000-calorie diet.

Measurements Conversions

tsp. – tea spoon   oz. – ounce   ml – milliliter
tbsp. – tablespoon   lb. – pound   g – grams
pt. – pint

Cups	Fluid oz.	Tablespoons
1 cup	8 oz.	16 tbsp.
¾ cup	6 oz.	12 tbsp.
⅔ cup	5 ⅓ oz.	10 tbsp. + 2 tsp.
½ cup	4 oz.	8 tbsp.
⅓ cup	2 ⅔ oz.	5 tbsp. + 1 tsp.
¼ cup	2 oz.	4 tbsp.
⅛ cup	1 oz.	2 tbsp.
1/16 cup	½ oz.	1 tbsp.

Cups to Milliliters

1 cup	240 ml
¾ cup	180 ml
⅔ cup	160 ml
½ cup	120 ml
⅓ cup	80 ml
¼ cup	60 ml
1 tbsp.	15 ml
1 tsp.	5 ml

Cups to Grams for Dry Goods

1 cup	127 g
⅔ cup	85 g
½ cup	64 g
⅓ cup	42 g
¼ cup	32 g
⅛ cup	32 g

Cups to Grams for some ingredients

1 cup flour	125 g
1 cup granulated sugar	201 g
1 cup butter	227 g
1 cup heavy cream	235 g

RECIPES

Baked Chicken Wings with the Dipping Sauce

Prep: 10 min
Cook Time: 35 min
Total time: 45 min
Servings: 2

> *Italian cooks prefer individual herbs rather than a blend. As an American invention, Italian seasoning is best used in the American versions of classic Italian dishes. And it works great as an all-purpose seasoning.*

Nutrition Facts Amount Per Serving

- Calories - 454
- Total Fat – 17.5 g
- Saturated Fat - 4.7 g
- Cholesterol - 202 mg
- Sodium - 1275 mg
- Potassium - 620 mg
- Total Carbohydrate - 3.7 g
- Dietary Fiber - 0.4 g
- Sugars - 1.1 g
- Protein - 67 g

Ingredients

- 1 lb. chicken wings
- 2 tbsp. soy sauce
- 2 tbsp. yellow mustard
- 2 cloves garlic, minced
- 1 tsp Italian herbs seasoning
- salt and black pepper to taste

Ingredients for the Dipping Sauce

- 4 tbsp. of mayonnaise, high-fat low-sugar
- 2 tbsp. reduced sugar ketchup. You can replace it with tomato paste
- 1 dash of black pepper

Steps/Directions:

1. Preheat the oven to 400°F. Season chicken wings with salt and black pepper.
2. Mix soy sauce, mustard, and garlic in a bowl. Add chicken wings to the sauce and coat them well.
3. Place the chicken wings on a lined baking sheet, sprinkle with Italian herbs seasoning, and bake for 30-35 mins.
4. Mix the ingredients for the dipping sauce. Serve the chicken wings with the sauce. Enjoy!

Baked Chicken with Garlic and Lemons

Prep: 20 min
Cook Time: 60 min
Total time: 80 min
Servings: 2

The name of the herb "oregano" meant "Joy of the Mountain" in Ancient Greek.

Dried oregano seasoning is used to enrich the flavor of meat and vegetable dishes.

Nutrition Facts Amount Per Serving

- Calories – 880
- Total Fat - 78.3 g
- Saturated Fat - 19.2 g
- Cholesterol - 172 mg
- Sodium - 988 mg
- Potassium - 279.7 mg
- Total Carbohydrate -18.7 g
- Dietary Fiber - 5.5 g
- Sugars - 8.8 g
- Protein – 31 g

Ingredients

- 1 lb. chicken thighs
- 3 tbsp. extra-virgin olive oil
- 4 cloves garlic, minced
- 1 tsp dried oregano
- ½ medium yellow onion, cut into wedges
- juice of 1 lemon
- ½ lb. asparagus, ends removed
- ½ cup chicken broth reduced sodium
- 2 tbsp. fresh parsley, chopped
- 1 lemon sliced
- salt and dash black pepper to taste
- ½ cup pitted Greek olives

Steps/Directions:

1. Season chicken with salt and pepper. Preheat the oven to 400°F.
2. Arrange onions in the baking pan.
3. Mix olive oil, garlic, lemon juice, and oregano.
4. Put the chicken on top of the onions and pour lemon-garlic sauce on top. Add chicken broth from the side of the pan; don't pour it on the chicken. Put the lemon slices on top of the chicken.
5. Bake uncovered for 45 mins.
6. Add asparagus to the pan on the sides, and Greek olives on top of the dish, and continue to bake for another 10 -15 mins.
7. Garnish with fresh parsley.

Baked Paprika Chicken Wings with Keto Ketchup

Prep: 10 min
Cook Time: 40 min
Total time: 50 min
Servings: 2

One tablespoon of paprika contains vitamins A and E, which protect vision, boost the immune system, and support organ health. Paprika also contains carotenoids which are a family of antioxidants.

Nutrition Facts Amount Per Serving

- Calories - 939
- Total Fat - 64.1 g
- Saturated Fat - 15.3 g
- Cholesterol - 179 mg
- Sodium - 1396 mg
- Potassium – 1256 mg
- Total Carbohydrate -43.4 g
- Dietary Fiber - 5.2 g
- Sugars -11 g
- Protein – 49 g

Ingredients

- 1 lb. chicken wings
- 2 tsp paprika
- ½ tsp salt
- 2 tbsp. olive oil

Ingredients for the Keto Ketchup

- 1 cup of water
- 6 oz. tomato paste
- 2 servings Stevia
- 1 tsp salt
- 3 tbsp. apple cider vinegar
- ½ tsp garlic powder
- ½ tsp onion powder
- ½ tsp paprika
- ¼ tsp cinnamon
- 1 dash of ground cloves

Steps/Directions:

1. Preheat the oven to 400 °F. Season chicken wings with salt and paprika.
2. Place the chicken wings on a lined baking sheet and drizzle them with oil. Bake for 35-40 mins.
3. In a saucepan, mix the ingredients for Keto ketchup and simmer over medium heat for 10 -15 mins until the ketchup thickens. You can keep it in your fridge in a container for up to 10 days.
4. Serve the chicken wings with ketchup.

Balsamic Cranberry Roast Chicken

Prep: 60 min
Cook Time: 40 min
Total time: 100 min
Servings: 2

> The herb rosemary retains its fragrance even when dried and stored in glass.
> In troubadours' songs and English medieval traditions, rosemary was an emblem of remembrance and fidelity. Rosemary can increase blood circulation, boost memory, reduce inflammation, and strengthen the immune system.

Nutrition Facts Amount Per Serving

- Calories – 701
- Total Fat - 44.7 g
- Saturated Fat -10.5 g
- Cholesterol - 208 mg
- Sodium – 1,528 mg
- Potassium - 687 mg
- Total Carbohydrate -29.6 g
- Dietary Fiber - 2.7 g
- Sugars - 3.1 g
- Protein - 60 g

Ingredients

- 1 lb. chicken thighs and drumsticks
- 1/3 cup balsamic vinegar
- 2 cloves garlic, minced
- 2 tbsp. extra-virgin olive oil
- 1 tbsp. reduced-sodium soy sauce
- 1 cup fresh cranberries, divided
- 1 tbsp. lemon juice
- 1 tsp dried oregano
- 1 tsp thyme leaves, chopped
- 1 tsp fresh rosemary, chopped
- zest of 1 orange
- salt and black pepper to taste
- 6 rosemary springs for garnish

Steps/Directions:

1. For marinade, mix in a food processor garlic, balsamic vinegar, olive oil, soy sauce, lemon juice, and a half of cranberries.
2. Place the chicken in a big bowl or a zip-lock bag, pour the marinade, and leave it in the fridge for 30-60 mins.
3. Preheat the oven to 400°F. Grease a roasting pan. Take the chicken from the marinade (preserve the marinade).
4. Place the chicken in the roasting pan, skin side down. Season it with salt, black pepper, oregano, thyme, and rosemary. Sprinkle with the remaining cranberries and orange zest. Roast for 25-30 mins. Flip over the chicken and brush it with the marinade.
5. Increase the oven temperature to 415°F and continue to roast for 8-10 mins until golden brown.
6. Garnish with fresh rosemary springs before serving.

Buffalo Chicken Celery Sticks

Prep: 10 min
Cook Time: 10 min
Total time: 20 min
Servings: 12

> *Blackstrap molasses is rich in iron. It is a great natural source of calcium, magnesium, and potassium.*
>
> *One tablespoon of blackstrap molasses has only 42 calories.*

Nutrition Facts Amount Per Serving

- Calories – 286
- Total Fat - 17.8 g
- Saturated Fat - 7.4 g
- Cholesterol – 125 mg
- Sodium - 162 mg
- Total Carbohydrate - 2.4 g
- Dietary Fiber - 0.2 g
- Sugars – 0.6 g
- Protein - 29 g

Ingredients

- 2 cups shredded rotisserie chicken (or leftover chicken)
- 2 tbsp. mayonnaise
- 2 tbsp. soft cream cheese
- 1 clove garlic, minced
- salt, and black pepper, ground to taste
- 3 tbsp of homemade keto buffalo sauce
- 6 celery stalks, cut in halves
- 2 tbsp. chives (or other greens for garnish), chopped

Ingredients for Homemade Keto Buffalo Sauce

- 4-5 tbsps. Your favorite hot sauce, low sugar
- 4 tbsps. unsalted butter
- 1 tsp blackstrap molasses
- ¼ tsp cayenne pepper (optional)
- 2 cloves garlic, minced

Steps/Directions:

1. In a big bowl mix the chicken with mayonnaise, cream cheese, garlic, and homemade keto buffalo sauce. Season everything with salt and black pepper.
2. Fill each half of a celery stalk with chicken filling and garnish with greens.

Chicken breasts stuffed with antipasti

Prep: 10 min
Cook Time: 30 min
Total time: 40 min
Servings: 4

Parmesan is very high in protein, vitamins, and minerals.

Parmesan is low in lactose so moderate portions of this cheese can often be tolerated by people with lactose intolerance.

Nutrition Facts Amount Per Serving

- Calories - 290
- Total Fat - 20.6 g
- Saturated Fat - 4.1 g
- Cholesterol – 82 mg
- Sodium – 558 mg
- Potassium - 99 mg
- Total Carbohydrate - 1.9 g
- Dietary Fiber - 0.4 g
- Sugars - 0.8 g
- Protein - 33 g

Ingredients

- 4 boneless skinless chicken breasts
- 2 tbsp. extra-virgin olive oil
- 1 tsp Italian herbs seasoning
- salt and black pepper to taste
- 2 slices of Genoa salami
- 2 slices of mozzarella cheese
- 2 sun-dried tomatoes, sliced
- 1/3 cup assorted olives, pitted sliced
- 2 tbsp. grated Parmesan cheese
- 2 tbsp. fresh parsley, chopped

Steps/Directions:

1. Preheat the oven to 400° F. Carefully make six slits in each breast, trying not to cut through.
2. Pour olive oil on a baking sheet, and place the chicken on it. Season chicken breasts with salt, pepper, and Italian herbs.
3. Insert in the slits in the chicken breasts the slices of salami, mozzarella cheese, sun-dried tomatoes, and olives. Sprinkle with Parmesan cheese.
4. Bake for 25-30 mins or until cooked through.
5. Garnish with fresh parsley and serve.

Chicken Breasts Stuffed with Broccoli and Cheese

Prep: 20 min
Cook Time: 30 min
Total time: 50 min
Servings: 2

> *Black Pepper is rich in vitamins A and C and has a very high caffeine content.*
>
> *Pastry chefs include black pepper in all kinds of desserts. It's an especially delicious surprise in chocolate sweets like brownies, chocolate cake, and truffles.*

Nutrition Facts Amount Per Serving

- Calories - 577.9
- Total Fat - 29.3 g
- Saturated Fat - 8.7 g
- Sodium – 923 mg
- Potassium - 733 mg
- Total Carbohydrate - 6.2 g
- Sugars - 1.8 g
- Protein - 34 g

Ingredients

- 2 chicken breasts
- 1 tsp Italian herbs seasoning
- 1/4 tsp turmeric
- 1/2 tsp salt, divided
- 1 dash of black pepper
- 2 tbsp. olive oil, divided
- 1 cup broccoli florets, chopped
- 3 oz. Bella mushrooms, sliced
- 1/3 cup mozzarella cheese, shredded
- ¼ cup grated Parmesan
- 1 clove of garlic, minced
- 1 tsp lemon juice

Steps/Directions:

1. Preheat the oven to 400°F.
2. Steam or boil broccoli florets for 2 mins, let them cool down and chop them.
3. Preheat a skillet; pour some olive oil, and add Bella mushrooms. Season with salt and cook for 4-5 mins.
4. Slice each chicken breast to make a pocket. Season chicken with salt, black pepper, turmeric, and Italian herbs.
5. In a bowl, combine broccoli, mushrooms, garlic, lemon juice, mozzarella, and Parmesan cheese. Stuff each chicken breast with the mixture.
6. Place the chicken breasts in a baking pan, sprinkle them with olive oil, cover them with aluminum foil, and bake for 20 mins or until cooked through. Uncover the chicken, and bake for another 5-7 mins until golden brown color.

Chicken Breasts Stuffed with Spinach and Feta Cheese

Prep: 15 min
Cook Time: 35 min
Total time: 50 min
Servings: 2

Turmeric will work better if you combine it with other spices and herbs like cinnamon, black pepper, and ginger.

Nutrition Facts Amount Per Serving

- Calories - 738.6
- Total Fat - 47.7 g
- Saturated Fat - 20.0 g
- Cholesterol -241.6 mg
- Sodium – 1,939.0 mg
- Potassium - 886.6 mg
- Total Carbohydrate -14.4 g
- Dietary Fiber – 6.1 g
- Sugars - 5.2 g
- Protein – 44 g

Ingredients

- 2 chicken breasts
- 1 cup frozen spinach, chopped
- 2 cloves garlic, minced
- 1/3 cup onion, chopped
- ½ cup feta cheese, crumbled
- 1/3 cup heavy cream or half-and-half
- 4 oz. cream cheese
- 1 tsp Italian herbs seasoning
- 1/4 tsp turmeric
- ½ tsp salt
- 1 dash of black pepper
- 2 tbsp. olive oil

Steps/Directions:

1. Preheat the oven to 400 °F.
2. Preheat a skillet, add frozen spinach and cook for 4-5 mins until it's soft. Add oil, onions, and garlic, season with salt and pepper, and cook for another 2 mins.
3. Add heavy cream, feta, and cream cheese to the spinach. Mix well to combine, cook for 2 mins until the mixture is thickened, and put the filling in a bowl.
4. Slice each chicken breast to make a pocket. Season chicken with salt, black pepper, turmeric, and Italian herbs.
5. Stuff each chicken breast with the filling.
6. Place the chicken breasts in a baking pan, sprinkle them with olive oil, cover with aluminum foil, and bake for 35-40 mins or until cooked through. Uncover the chicken, and bake for another 5-7 mins until golden brown color.

Chicken Creamy Broccoli Casserole

Prep: 15 min
Cook Time: 40 min
Total time: 55 min
Servings: 4

Pesto is a sauce that originated in Liguria, Italy. It is made of crushed basil. Other ingredients are garlic, olive oil, salt, pine nuts, and certain kinds of cheese (most often Parmesan cheese, Pecorino Sardo or Pecorino Romano). You can also add black pepper if you want.

Nutrition Facts Amount Per Serving

- Calories - 654
- Total Fat - 43.3 g
- Saturated Fat - 22.3 g
- Cholesterol - 289 mg
- Sodium - 1157 mg
- Potassium - 413 mg
- Total Carbohydrate -11.5 g
- Dietary Fiber - 2.8 g
- Sugars - 4.4 g
- Protein - 57 g

Ingredients

- 2 lb. chicken thigh, skinless, boneless, cut into small pieces
- ½ cup cream cheese
- 1 cups cheddar cheese, shredded
- ½ cup heavy whipping cream or half-and-half
- 3 tbsp. green pesto
- 1 tbsp. lime juice
- 2 tbsp. butter, unsalted
- 2 tbsp. onions, chopped
- 2 cloves garlic, minced
- 1 orange bell pepper, sliced
- 4 oz. cherry tomatoes cut in halves
- ½ lb. broccoli florets
- 1 tsp salt
- 1 dash of black pepper
- 1 tsp oregano
- 1 tsp dried thyme

Steps/Directions:

1. Preheat the oven to 400°F.
2. In a frying pan, melt butter, add the chicken pieces, season with salt, and black pepper, and cook for 5-6 mins until golden brown color. Add onions, and continue to cook for 2 mins. Add garlic and cook for another 1 min.
3. In a bowl, mix cream (or half-and-half) with cream cheese, pesto, and lime juice. Season with salt to taste.
4. Place the chicken in the baking pan, and add broccoli, bell pepper, and tomatoes. Season with oregano and dried thyme, and pour the creamy sauce on top.
5. Sprinkle cheddar cheese on top, cover the baking pan with aluminum foil, and bake for 45 mins. Uncover the baking pan and bake for another 5-6 mins until golden crust.

Chicken Creamy Soup

Prep: 10 min
Cook Time: 15 min
Total time: 25 min
Servings: 6

The spice oregano is known for its aroma and slightly bitter flavor. It is usually used in its dry form, as the aromas of fresh oregano are highly pungent and can easily overpower a dish.

Nutrition Facts Amount Per Serving

- Calories - 425
- Total Fat - 27.5 g
- Saturated Fat - 16.9 g
- Cholesterol - 133.9 mg
- Sodium - 841 mg
- Potassium - 360 mg
- Total Carbohydrate – 5 g
- Dietary Fiber - 1.1 g
- Sugars - 1.9 g
- Protein - 35 g

Ingredients

- 3 cups shredded cooked chicken
- 2 cloves garlic, minced
- 2 tbsp. onions, chopped
- 1 bell pepper, diced
- 1 carrot, sliced
- 3 cups baby spinach, chopped
- 2 tbsp. butter, unsalted
- 8 oz. soft cream cheese
- ¾ cup Parmesan cheese, grated
- 4 cups of water
- ½ tsp salt
- 1 dash of black pepper
- 1 tsp oregano
- 1 tsp dried basil
- 2 tbsp. fresh parsley, chopped
- 2 tbsp. blue cheese, crumbled (optional)

Steps/Directions:

1. Preheat a large pot, melt butter, and add baby spinach. Cook for 3 mins. Then add onions, carrot, bell pepper, and garlic and cook for another 2 mins.
2. Add cream cheese and Parmesan cheese and stir for 1 min.
3. Add water and chicken, and season with salt, black pepper, dried basil, and oregano. Bring to boiling and cook for 5-6 mins, stirring occasionally.
4. Garnish with parsley and crumbled blue cheese.

Chicken Drumsticks baked

Prep: 10 min
Cook Time: 45 min
Total time: 55 min
Servings: 2

> *Dried thyme retains much of the flavor of the fresh herb. When substituting dried thyme for fresh, use about one-third of fresh thyme volume called for in the recipe as the flavor of dried thyme is much stronger than fresh.*

Nutrition Facts Amount Per Serving

- Calories - 315.9
- Total Fat - 21.1 g
- Saturated Fat - 4.8 g
- Cholesterol - 105.8 mg
- Sodium - 660 mg
- Potassium - 311.8 mg
- Total Carbohydrate - 4 g
- Dietary Fiber - 1.3 g
- Sugars - 0.9 g
- Protein - 26.1 g

Ingredients

- 4 medium chicken drumsticks
- 2 tbsp. avocado oil
- 1/2 tsp turmeric
- 1 tsp dried basil
- 1 tsp dried thyme
- 1 tbsp. heavy cream
- 1 tsp garlic powder
- 1 tsp onion powder
- ½ tsp salt
- ½ tsp black pepper

Steps/Directions:

1. Preheat your oven to 400 °F.
2. In a small bowl mix all the ingredients of the marinade. Pour the marinade into a Ziploc plastic bag and place the chicken drumsticks into it. Make sure the chicken is covered well with the marinade. You can leave the chicken in the plastic bag in the fridge for 30 mins. Or you can cook it right away.
3. Place the chicken in a baking pan and cook for 45 mins.

Chicken in Wine (Coq au Vin)

Prep: 30 min
Cook Time: 60 min
Total time: 90 min
Servings: 6

> *Herbes de Provence traditionally includes thyme, basil, rosemary, tarragon, savory, marjoram, oregano, and bay leaf.*
>
> *Julia Child is credited with defining the mixture and adding it to the culinary lexicon of chefs all over the world.*

Nutrition Facts Amount Per Serving

- Calories - 427.8
- Total Fat - 27.3 g
- Saturated Fat - 9.1 g
- Cholesterol - 107 mg
- Sodium - 900 mg
- Total Carbohydrate - 10.1 g
- Dietary Fiber - 1.6 g
- Sugars - 3.5 g
- Protein - 22 g

Ingredients

- 6 chicken legs on the bone (thighs and drumsticks)
- 3 strips of bacon, chopped
- 1 onion, chopped
- 3 cloves garlic, minced
- 6 oz. Baby Bella mushrooms, sliced
- 3 medium carrots, round sliced
- 2 tbsp. olive oil
- ½ tsp salt
- 1 dash of black pepper
- 2 tsp Herbes de Provence seasoning
- 2 cups dry red wine
- 1 cup of water
- 1 cup whipping cream
- 2 tbsp. fresh parsley, chopped (steamed broccoli or thyme for garnish)

Steps/Directions:

1. Preheat a large skillet, and add 1 tbsp. of olive oil and cook chicken for 5-6 mins per side until golden brown. Remove the chicken to a plate.
2. Now in the same skillet, cook the bacon for 7-8 mins until fully cooked. Then place the bacon on a paper towel. When it's cooled down, chop it.
3. To the same skillet, add onions and carrots and cook for 6-7 mins, then add garlic and cook for another 1 min. Add chicken and bacon, season with salt, pepper, and Herbes de Provence, pour wine and water and bring to a boil. Then simmer for 45 mins on low heat.
4. In another skillet, pour some olive oil and cook mushrooms for 5-6 mins. Then add whipping cream and simmer for another 5 mins.
5. Add creamy mushrooms to the chicken and continue to cook for another 10-15 mins.
6. Garnish with parsley and serve with your favorite green salad.

Chicken Lettuce Wraps

Prep: 10 min
Cook Time: 20 min
Total time: 30 min
Servings: 4

Parsley is high in vitamins A and C, fiber, potassium, magnesium, calcium, and iron. You may be surprised, but parsley is an excellent source of protein.

Nutrition Facts Amount Per Serving

- Calories – 364
- Total Fat - 27.1 g
- Saturated Fat - 7.3 g
- Cholesterol - 61 mg
- Sodium - 244 mg
- Potassium - 489.7 mg
- Total Carbohydrate - 8.7 g
- Dietary Fiber - 4.1 g
- Sugars - 1.4 g
- Protein - 26 g

Ingredients

- 1 lb. boneless and skinless chicken (breasts or thighs)
- 3 tbsp. olive oil, divided
- 2 cloves garlic, minced
- 1 tsp Italian herbs seasoning
- 8 leaves of lettuce
- 1 avocado, diced
- 1 tomato, diced
- 2 tbsp. onions, chopped
- 3-4 radishes, sliced
- 3 tbsp. red cabbage, chopped
- ½ cup parsley
- ½ cup sour cream or plain yogurt
- ½ lime juice
- salt and black pepper to taste

Steps/Directions:

1. Preheat a frying pan and pour some olive oil. Cut the chicken into bite pieces and add to the frying pan. Season with salt, black pepper, and Italian herbs seasoning. Cook for about 15-18 mins until the chicken is fully cooked.
2. Place parsley, sour cream or yogurt, lime juice, and 2 tbsp. of olive oil and garlic in your food processor, season with salt, and make a creamy sauce.
3. In a bowl, combine chicken with avocado, tomato, onions, red cabbage, and radishes.
4. Spoon the salad on each lettuce leaf and drizzle with the creamy sauce.

Chicken Meatballs with Flavored Melt Butter inside

Prep: 40 min
Cook Time: 25 min
Total time: 65 min
Servings: 4

Dill is used as an anti-bacterial spice, similar to garlic.

Because of its delicate nature, most chefs add fresh herbs to their hot recipes just before removing them from the heat.

Nutrition Facts Amount Per Serving

- Calories – 536
- Total Fat - 36.8 g
- Saturated Fat - 15.7 g
- Cholesterol – 188 mg
- Sodium – 386 mg
- Potassium - 541 mg
- Total Carbohydrate -17.8 g
- Dietary Fiber - 1.8 g
- Sugars - 1.5 g
- Protein – 38 g

Ingredients

- 1 lb. ground chicken
- 1 tsp Italian seasoning
- salt and black pepper to taste
- 2 tbsp. onions, chopped
- 1 egg
- 1/2 cup fresh chopped dill
- 6 tbsp. salted butter
- 3 cloves garlic, minced
- 2/3 cup panko or coconut flour (low-carb substitute for breadcrumbs)
- 2 tbsp. olive oil

Steps/Directions:

1. In a bowl, mix softened butter, dill, and garlic. Put the batter on a plastic wrap, roll it into a small log, and put it in the freezer for 30-35 min.
2. Mix ground chicken, egg, salt, black pepper, Italian seasoning, and onions.
3. Form 4 patties.
4. Take the butter from the freezer and cut it into four pieces.
5. Put one piece of butter on top of each patty and form the meatballs. The butter must be inside each meatball.
6. Coat each meatball in panko or coconut flour.
7. Pour olive oil into a skillet, place the meatballs there, and cook over medium heat for 5-6 min per each side until a golden crust.

Chicken Meatballs with Marinara sauce

Prep: 10 min
Cook Time: 30 min
Total time: 40 min
Servings: 2

Cinnamon isn't just for dessert! It's been used to flavor meat for thousands of years. The recipes of Moroccan chicken, chickpea, or lamb tagine all require cinnamon. Cinnamon helps to balance the richness of buttery meat.

Nutrition Facts Amount Per Serving

- Calories – 705
- Total Fat - 42.1 g
- Saturated Fat - 10.7 g
- Cholesterol – 297 mg
- Sodium – 1231 mg
- Potassium - 859 mg
- Total Carbohydrate -11.6 g
- Dietary Fiber - 2.5 g
- Sugars - 6.4 g
- Protein – 74 g

Ingredients

- 1 lb. ground chicken
- 1 tsp Italian seasoning
- ½ tsp salt
- 1 dash of black pepper
- ½ tsp cinnamon
- 2 tbsp. onions, chopped
- 1 egg
- 2 tbsp. Parmesan cheese, grated
- 1/3 cup fresh parsley, chopped
- 1 clove of garlic, minced
- 2 tbsp. olive oil
- ½ cup Marinara sauce

Steps/Directions:

1. Preheat the oven to 400°F.
2. Preheat a skillet and add olive oil. Add garlic and onion and cook over medium heat for 1-2 mins until fragrant.
3. Season ground chicken with salt, pepper, cinnamon, and Italian seasoning. Add garlic with onions, egg, Parmesan cheese, and parsley (leave a small amount for topping). Mix well.
4. Form meatballs and place them into a baking pan. Pour Marinara sauce on top of the chicken meatballs. Bake for 30 mins. Add a little bit of water to the baking pan if needed.
5. Garnish with fresh parsley and serve with your favorite salad.

Creamy Chicken with Mushrooms

Prep: 10 min
Cook Time: 20 min
Total time: 30 min
Servings: 4

> *Garlic is a natural antibiotic and antifungal that may reduce "bad" cholesterol.*
>
> *If garlic has been cooked too long or at too high of a temperature, it will turn bitter.*

Nutrition Facts Amount Per Serving

- Calories - 445.1
- Total Fat – 32.4 g
- Saturated Fat - 9.5 g
- Cholesterol – 71 mg
- Sodium - 526 mg
- Potassium - 470 mg
- Total Carbohydrate - 20.6 g
- Dietary Fiber - 2.5 g
- Sugars - 1.7 g
- Protein – 20 g

Ingredients

- 1 lb. of chicken tenders
- ½ lb. mushrooms, sliced
- 2 tbsp. extra-virgin olive oil
- 2 tbsp. butter unsalted
- 2 cloves garlic, minced
- 2 tbsp. onions, chopped
- 2 tbsp. fresh parsley, chopped
- ½ cup of water
- ½ cup heavy cream or half-and-half
- 2 tbsp. sour cream
- salt and black pepper to taste
- 1/4 tsp turmeric, ground
- 1 tsp Italian herbs seasoning

Steps/Directions:

1. Preheat a frying pan, pour some olive oil and unsalted butter and add the chicken tenders. Season with salt, black pepper, turmeric, and Italian herbs seasoning, and cook for 5 mins on each side. Then remove the chicken from the frying pan.

2. Add some olive oil to the same frying pan and add the mushrooms. Cook them on medium-high heat until all the liquid is gone, and the mushrooms get a nice brown color (for about 5-6 mins). Add onions and season with salt to your taste. Cook for another two mins. Add garlic and cook for one more minute.

3. Add water, heavy cream or half-and-half, sour cream, and parsley, and cook until the sauce starts to thicken.

4. Return the chicken to the pan and coat it well with the sauce. Cook for three more minutes and serve.

Chicken Pan with Vegetables

Prep: 15 min
Cook Time: 50 min
Total time: 65 min
Servings: 4

Sesame oil is used for tempering as a flavor enhancer. It is enriched with vitamins and minerals. Take a bottle of sesame oil and shake it gently. If the bubble is transparent and disappears quickly, this indicates that the sesame oil is pure and of good quality.

Nutrition Facts Amount Per Serving

- Calories – 438
- Total Fat - 15 g
- Saturated Fat - 6.7 g
- Cholesterol – 205 mg
- Sodium – 734 mg
- Potassium - 1333 mg
- Total Carbohydrate - 20.7 g
- Dietary Fiber - 7.2 g
- Sugar - 10.6 g
- Protein - 71 g

Ingredients

- 2 lb. boneless, skinless chicken breasts
- 1 tbsp. sesame oil
- 2 tbsp. soy sauce
- 1/4 tsp turmeric
- 2 red bell peppers, diced
- 3 carrots, sliced
- 1 large zucchini, sliced
- 1 small eggplant, diced
- 3 tbsp. red onion, diced
- 2 tbsp. extra-virgin olive oil
- salt and black pepper to taste
- 2 cloves garlic, minced
- 1 tbsp. Parmesan cheese, grated
- ½ cup mozzarella cheese, grated
- 2 tbsp. fresh parsley, chopped or fresh rosemary

Steps/Directions:

1. Preheat the oven to 400°F. Drizzle a baking sheet with olive oil.
2. Season chicken with salt and black pepper, and place it on the baking sheet. In a bowl, mix sesame oil, soy sauce, and turmeric, and pour the mixture on top of the chicken. Use a brush to spread the sauce evenly.
3. Place the vegetables on the baking sheet around the chicken: red bell peppers, carrots, zucchini, eggplant, and onions.
4. Whisk together olive oil, salt, and garlic. Drizzle the vegetables with it.
5. Sprinkle everything with mozzarella and Parmesan cheese.
6. Bake for 45 - 50 mins until the chicken is fully cooked and the vegetables are soft and tender.
7. Garnish with parsley or rosemary and serve.

Chicken Parmesan Casserole with Spaghetti Squash

Prep: 15 min
Cook Time: 30 min
Total time: 45 min
Servings: 4

Spaghetti squash contains nine minerals that contribute to bone health, and it is rich in manganese.

Nutrition Facts Amount Per Serving

- Calories – 782
- Total Fat - 32.8 g
- Saturated Fat - 9.2 g
- Cholesterol – 254 mg
- Sodium – 1321 mg
- Potassium - 761 mg
- Total Carbohydrate - 27.1 g
- Dietary Fiber - 8.2 g
- Sugars - 4.5 g
- Protein - 87 g

Ingredients

- 2 lb. chicken, boneless and skinless
- 1 egg
- ½ cup coconut flour or almond flour
- ¼ cup Parmesan cheese, grated
- 1 tsp salt, divided
- 1 dash of black pepper
- 1 tsp Italian herbs seasoning
- 3 tbsp. olive oil, divided
- 4 cups spaghetti squash, cooked and well drained
- 1 clove of garlic, minced
- 3 tbsp. pine nuts, toasted
- 2/3 cup low-sugar marinara sauce
- 6 oz. mozzarella cheese, grated or sliced
- 2 tbsp. basil or parsley, chopped for garnish

Steps/Directions:

1. Cut the meat into small cube pieces.
2. Beat the egg in a bowl. In another bowl, mix the flour, salt, black pepper, Parmesan cheese, and Italian herbs seasoning.
3. Heat the oil in a skillet. Dip each piece of chicken in the egg and then in the flour-spices mixture and place in the skillet. Cook the chicken for 5-7 mins on each side until golden brown.
4. Preheat the oven to 385°F. Spread the squash spaghetti in a baking pan. Season with salt, black pepper, garlic, and drizzle with olive oil and pine nuts.
5. Put the chicken on top of the squash spaghetti. Cover everything with the marinara sauce and sprinkle with mozzarella cheese.
6. Bake for 30 mins. Garnish with fresh greens.

Chicken Parmesan Stuffed Peppers

Prep: 10 min
Cook Time: 25 min
Total time: 35 min
Servings: 4

Awaken your morning coffee or tea by adding a pinch of cinnamon to it.

You can also add a few drops of cinnamon oil to your sunscreen or lotion to prevent bugs from biting you.

Nutrition Facts Amount Per Serving

- Calories - 257.7
- Total Fat - 13.2 g
- Saturated Fat - 2.5 g
- Cholesterol - 81.6 mg
- Sodium - 339.5 mg
- Potassium - 364 mg
- Total Carbohydrate -10 g
- Dietary Fiber - 1.9 g
- Sugars – 6 g
- Protein -19.2 g

Ingredients

- 8 oz. ground chicken
- 2 bell peppers, red and yellow
- ½ cup marinara sauce, low sugar
- ¾ cup mozzarella cheese
- 2 tbsp. onions, chopped
- 2 cloves garlic, minced
- 2 tbsp. extra-virgin olive oil
- ½ tsp cinnamon
- 1 dash of salt
- 1 dash of black pepper
- 1/3 cup of water

Steps/Directions:

1. Preheat the oven to 385°F.
2. Cut the bell peppers in halves lengthwise, clean, and wash inside. Place peppers in a baking pan.
3. Pour some oil into a frying pan and cook garlic and onions for about 2 mins until fragrant. Add ground chicken. Season with salt, pepper, and cinnamon. Add marinara sauce, and one-half mozzarella cheese, and mix everything well. Cook for about 5 mins.
4. Stuff peppers with chicken and top with the remaining mozzarella cheese.
5. Add some water to the baking pan and cover it with aluminum foil. Bake for 25 mins and serve.

Chicken patties with Bella Mushrooms

Prep: 15 min
Cook Time: 10 min
Total time: 25 min
Servings: 6

> You shouldn't chop parsley for garnish too finely — bigger pieces are prettier and have more flavor.
>
> Ten sprigs of parsley are enough to reach the recommended daily intake of vitamin K.

Nutrition Facts Amount Per Serving

- Calories - 165
- Total Fat - 11.2 g
- Saturated Fat - 3.4 g
- Cholesterol - 45 mg
- Sodium - 206 mg
- Potassium - 159 mg
- Total Carbohydrate - 1.9 g
- Dietary Fiber - 0.2 g
- Sugars - 0.9 g
- Protein - 15 g

Ingredients

- ½ pound ground chicken
- 2 tbsp. onions, chopped
- 1 clove of garlic, minced
- ½ tsp cinnamon
- 1 tsp Italian herbs seasoning
- 1 tbsp. fresh parsley, chopped
- 2 tbsp. olive oil
- 1 tbsp. grated Parmesan cheese
- salt and black pepper to taste
- 3 oz. Bella mushrooms
- 1 tbsp. sour cream

Steps/Directions:

1. Cut off the caps of 12 mushrooms. Season with salt and put them on a lined baking sheet. Bake in the oven at 385°F for 10 mins.
2. Chop the stems of the mushrooms.
3. Season ground chicken with salt, pepper, Italian seasoning, and cinnamon. Then add onions, garlic, parsley, Parmesan cheese, sour cream, and chopped mushrooms. Mix to combine.
4. Heat olive oil in a skillet over medium heat. Form 6 patties and place them into the skillet. Cook for about 3-4 mins per side.
5. Take the mushrooms' caps out of the oven. Assemble mini-burgers by placing one chicken patty between two mushrooms' caps.
6. Garnish with fresh parsley and serve with your favorite salad.

Chicken Pot Pie

Prep: 30 min
Cook Time: 25 min
Total time: 55 min
Servings: 4

Coconut flour is an excellent alternative to wheat flour.

Coconut flour is thicker than wheat flour and requires more liquids. Because it is gluten-free, doughs made with coconut flour need to be mixed longer.

Nutrition Facts Amount Per Serving

- Calories - 618.3
- Total Fat - 29 g
- Saturated Fat - 13.6 g
- Cholesterol – 279 mg
- Sodium – 235 mg
- Potassium - 1192 mg
- Total Carbohydrate - 30.7 g
- Dietary Fiber - 15.1 g
- Sugars - 3.6 g
- Protein - 61 g

Ingredients

- 2 lb. chicken breasts; cut into cubes
- 3 tbsp. butter, unsalted
- ½ cup onions, chopped
- 1 small carrot, sliced
- 2 clove garlic, minced
- 1 tsp Italian herbs seasoning
- 1 tbsp. lemon juice
- 1 cup water
- 1 cup frozen green peas
- ½ cup heavy cream
- salt and black pepper to taste
- 1 ½ cup mozzarella cheese, shredded
- 1 cup coconut flour
- 1 tbsp. flax meal
- 1 tsp baking powder
- 2 tbsp. sour cream
- 1 egg and 1 egg mixed with 1 tbsp. water

Steps/Directions:

1. Preheat the oven to 400°F and grease a baking pan.
2. In a skillet, melt butter over medium heat and add onions and carrots. Cook for 4-5 mins. Then add garlic and cook for one more min.
3. Stir in water and lemon juice and simmer for 5 mins.
4. Add heavy cream and green peas. Simmer on low heat until the sauce is thick. Add some salt and pepper if needed.
5. Add chicken pieces, coat them well with the sauce, and season with salt, black pepper, and Italian herbs. Simmer for 3-4 mins and remove to the baking pan.
6. Make the crust: melt mozzarella cheese and mix it with sour cream, egg, coconut flour, flax meal, baking powder, and salt. Make dough.
7. Spread the dough over the filling covering the baking pan and folding it down around the edges. Cut the letter X on top of the crust and brush with the egg-water mixture.
8. Bake for 20-25 minutes or until the crust is golden brown.

Chicken Ranch Casserole

Prep: 25 min
Cook Time: 20 min
Total time: 45 min
Servings: 8

Fresh spinach loses its vitamins over time. Frozen spinach keeps the nutrients packed inside. That's why it's always good to keep it in your freezer.

Nutrition Facts Amount Per Serving

- Calories - 463
- Total Fat - 26.4 g
- Saturated Fat - 10.6 g
- Cholesterol - 149 mg
- Sodium - 842.1 mg
- Potassium - 731 mg
- Total Carbohydrate - 4.6 g
- Dietary Fiber - 1.4 g
- Sugars - 1.3 g
- Protein - 47 g

Ingredients

- 2 lb. chicken breasts
- 8 slices of bacon
- 2 cloves garlic, minced
- ¾ cup Ranch dressing
- 1 cup Mozzarella cheese, shredded
- 1 cup Cheddar cheese, shredded
- ½ cup heavy cream or half–and–half
- 1 lb. frozen spinach, chopped
- 2 tbsp. extra-virgin olive oil
- 2 tbsp. onions, chopped
- salt and black pepper to taste
- 1 tsp Italian herbs seasoning
- 2 tbsp. fresh parsley, chopped

Steps/Directions:

1. Preheat the oven to 400°F.
2. Preheat a large skillet and pour some olive oil. Season the chicken breasts with salt, black pepper, and Italian herbs seasoning and cook for 4-5 mins on each side. Then remove the chicken to a plate and let it cool down.
3. In the same skillet, cook bacon until it is fully cooked. Then place the bacon slices on a plate.
4. Now, use the skillet for cooking frozen spinach for 5-6 mins. Then pour some olive oil, add onions, and cook for 2 mins, add garlic and cook for 1 min.
5. Cut the chicken into cubes and chop the bacon slices. Put everything in a baking casserole dish and combine with spinach, Ranch dressing, Mozzarella, Cheddar cheese (leave some cheese for topping), heavy cream, or half-and-half. Mix well.
6. Top with remaining cheese and bake for 15-20 mins. Garnish with fresh parsley.

Chicken Breasts with Zucchini, Tomatoes, and Mozzarella

Prep: 15 min
Cook Time: 25 min
Total time: 40 min
Servings: 4

Black Pepper loses its flavor and aroma through evaporation. Keep it in an airtight container and out of the sun.

Nutrition Facts Amount Per Serving

- Calories - 393.7
- Total Fat - 14.9 g
- Saturated Fat - 1.9 g
- Cholesterol - 109.8 mg
- Sodium - 170 mg
- Potassium - 228 mg
- Total Carbohydrate - 5.7 g
- Dietary Fiber - 1.2 g
- Sugars - 3.8 g
- Protein – 49 g

Ingredients

- 4 boneless skinless chicken breasts
- 1 baby zucchini, halved and sliced
- 3 plum tomatoes, sliced into half-moons
- ½ cup Mozzarella cheese, sliced
- 3 tbsp. extra-virgin olive oil
- 1 tsp Italian herbs seasoning
- salt and black pepper to taste
- 1 tbsp. lemon juice
- 2 cloves garlic, minced
- 2 tbsp. fresh parsley or basil, chopped

Steps/Directions:

1. Preheat the oven to 400°F. Carefully make six slits in each breast, trying not to cut through.
2. In a small bowl, mix 1 tbsp. of olive oil, garlic, and lemon juice. Brush the chicken with this mixture.
3. Pour some olive oil into a baking pan and, place the chicken on it. Season chicken breasts with salt, black pepper, and Italian herbs.
4. Insert in the slits in the chicken breasts the slices of tomatoes, zucchini, and Mozzarella cheese.
5. Bake for 25-30 mins.
6. Garnish with fresh parsley or basil and serve.

Chicken Thighs Baked in Tomato Sauce

Prep: 15 min
Cook Time: 25 min
Total time: 40 min
Servings: 4

Fresh dill is often added to seafood dishes, yogurt sauces, vinegar, salads, and soups, and it can also be used as a garnish like parsley.

Dill herb contains the elements that may help strengthen bones.

Nutrition Facts Amount Per Serving

- Calories – 492
- Total Fat - 30.1 g
- Saturated Fat - 8.5 g
- Cholesterol - 185 mg
- Sodium - 768 mg
- Potassium - 107 mg
- Total Carbohydrate - 4.4 g
- Dietary Fiber - 0.9 g
- Sugars - 2.5 g
- Protein - 38.2 g

Ingredients

- 4 bone-in skin-on chicken thighs
- 2 cloves garlic, minced
- 2 tbsp. onions, chopped
- 1 tbsp. extra-virgin olive oil
- ¾ cup low-sodium chicken broth
- ½ tsp salt
- 1 dash black pepper
- 2 tbsp. sour cream
- 2 tbsp. tomato paste
- 1 red bell pepper, sliced
- 2 tbsp. grated Parmesan cheese
- 1 tbsp. fresh basil or dill, chopped

Steps/Directions:

1. Preheat the oven to 400°F. Season the chicken with salt and black pepper. Pour olive oil into an oven-proven skillet and roast the chicken for 5 min per side. Put chicken aside on a plate.
2. In the same skillet, cook onions and bell pepper for 2-3 mins. Then add garlic and cook until fragrant, for 2 mins maximum.
3. Add broth, sour cream, and tomato paste, and season with more salt. Mix everything well. Bring to a simmer and put the chicken in the sauce.
4. Sprinkle with Parmesan cheese.
5. Put the skillet in the oven and bake uncovered for 20-25 mins.
6. Garnish with fresh basil or dill and serve.

Chicken Thighs baked with Eggplant and Cheese

Prep: 15 min
Cook Time: 20 min
Total time: 35 min
Servings: 2

> *It would be best if you don't separate the thyme leaves from the stem. When adding a whole sprig of thyme to a recipe, the leaves usually fall off during cooking. You can remove the stem before serving.*

Nutrition Facts Amount Per Serving

- Calories – 613
- Total Fat - 34 g
- Saturated Fat - 10.1 g
- Cholesterol - 219 mg
- Sodium - 1189 mg
- Potassium - 589 mg
- Total Carbohydrate - 18.3 g
- Dietary Fiber - 8.9 g
- Sugars - 8.3 g
- Protein - 63 g

Ingredients

- 2 Boneless Skinless Chicken thighs
- 1 medium eggplant
- 2 tbsp. extra-virgin olive oil
- 1 tsp dried oregano
- ½ tsp dried thyme
- ½ tsp salt
- 1 dash black pepper
- 2 tbsp. Marinara sauce
- 4 tbsp. Mozzarella cheese

Steps/Directions:

1. Preheat the oven to 400°F. Slice the eggplant into thick round slices and arrange them on a lined baking sheet. Season the eggplant with salt, black pepper, and oregano. Drizzle it with olive oil.
2. Pound chicken thighs and slice them into several slices equal to eggplant slices. Season chicken well with salt and black pepper.
3. Add some olive oil to a frying pan and put the chicken there. Cook chicken for about 3-4 mins per side.
4. Place one piece of chicken on one slice of eggplant.
5. Cover every portion with Marinara sauce and grated mozzarella cheese. Season with dried thyme.
6. Bake for 15 mins until the cheese turns golden brown. Serve with roasted vegetables or your favorite salad.

Chicken baked with Orange Sweet and Sour Sauce

Prep: 10 min
Cook Time: 20 min
Total time: 30 min
Servings: 3

Flax seeds' health benefits are attributed to the omega-3 fatty acids, lignans, and fiber they contain.

In the keto diet, flax seed meal is used for thickening a sauce.

Nutrition Facts Amount Per Serving

- Calories - 380.1
- Total Fat – 24.0 g
- Saturated Fat - 4.8 g
- Cholesterol – 196 mg
- Sodium – 1397 mg
- Potassium - 459 mg
- Total Carbohydrate - 13.6 g
- Dietary Fiber - 2.4 g
- Sugars - 7.3 g
- Protein – 27 g

Ingredients

- 1 lb. chicken boneless skinless thighs or tenders, cut into bite pieces
- ½ tsp salt
- 1 dash black pepper
- 1 tsp baking powder
- 1 egg
- 2 tbsp. olive oil
- 1 red bell pepper, diced
- 1 small onion, cut into wedges

Sweet and Sour Sauce

- fresh juice of 1 orange
- ¼ cup white vinegar
- 2 tbsp. Keto ketchup (check the recipe on the 8th page)
- 1 clove garlic, minced
- ½ tsp ground ginger
- 6 packages of stevia
- 1 tbsp. soy sauce
- 1 tbsp. ground flax seeds
- 4 tbsp. water
- 1 tbsp. sesame seeds
- 2 tbsp. scallions, chopped for garnish

Steps/Directions:

1. In a bowl, mix one egg, salt, black pepper, and baking powder, and whisk well.
2. Add the chicken to the mixture and coat well.
3. Preheat a frying pan and pour 2 tbsp. of olive oil. Add chicken and fry it in the hot oil for 3-4 mins until crispy. Move the chicken to a plate.
4. In the same pan add onions, and bell pepper, and sauté for 3-4 minutes until softened. Add all the sauce ingredients (fresh orange juice, white vinegar, ketchup, garlic, ginger, stevia, soy sauce). Bring to a simmer.
5. In a small bowl, mix the ground flax seeds with 4 tbsp. of water and add the mixture to the sauce. Continue to simmer for 2-3 minutes, until the sauce is thick enough.
6. Add chicken to the pan and coat it well with the sauce.
7. Garnish with sesame seeds and scallions and serve.

Rotisserie Stuffed Chicken

Prep: 20 min
Cook Time: 75 min
Total time: 95 min
Servings: 6

Sage is known for its robust flavor and aroma. That's why it's better to add sage early in the cooking process, rather than at the end like many other delicate herbs.
Sage oil can be applied to hair or skin to cleanse the area and regulate oil production.

Nutrition Facts Amount Per Serving

- Calories – 1088
- Total Fat - 98.3 g
- Saturated Fat – 14.4 g
- Cholesterol - 129.5 mg
- Sodium – 839 mg
- Potassium - 838 mg
- Total Carbohydrate - 20.1 g
- Dietary Fiber – 13.4 g
- Sugars - 5.7 g
- Protein – 43 g

Ingredients

- 1 whole chicken, medium size
- 1 clove garlic, minced
- 1/2 tsp. turmeric powder
- 1 tsp. dried parsley
- 1 tsp. dried thyme
- ½ tsp. dried rosemary
- 1 tsp. sage
- 3 tbsp. butter, divided
- 1 tsp. garlic paste
- 2 tbsp. onions, chopped
- 5 oz. mushrooms, sliced
- ½ cup pecans or pistachios, chopped
- 2 strips of bacon, chopped
- 1 egg
- 2 tbsp. almond meal
- ¼ cup sugar-free dried cranberries
- · salt and black pepper to taste

Steps/Directions:

1. Preheat the oven to 400°F. Season the chicken inside and outside with salt and pepper.
2. In a small bowl, mix 1 tbsp. of melt butter, turmeric powder, garlic, salt, and black pepper, and brush the skin of the chicken with the mixture.
3. Preheat a skillet and melt the butter, then add garlic paste and onions and sauté until softened. Add mushrooms and cook for 2 mins on medium heat.
4. Add bacon and pecans (or pistachios) and continue to cook for another 3-4 mins. Season everything with parsley, thyme, rosemary, and sage, cook for another 30 seconds, and turn off the heat.
5. In a mixing bowl, combine the stuffing with an egg, cranberries, and almond meal. Mix everything well and stuff the chicken.
6. Tie the chicken's legs with the rotisserie twine and place the chicken in a baking pan.
7. Roast for 1 hour 15 mins.

Chicken with Prunes and Dried Apricots

Prep: 20 min
Cook Time: 25 min
Total time: 35 min
Servings: 2

Bay Leaf contains proteins named enzymes that help digest food faster.

Also, bay leaves will enhance the taste of your meals without adding sodium.

Nutrition Facts Amount Per Serving

- Calories – 662
- Total Fat - 31.3 g
- Saturated Fat - 6.7 g
- Cholesterol - 202 mg
- Sodium - 799 mg
- Potassium - 984 mg
- Total Carbohydrate -32.6 g
- Dietary Fiber - 3.7 g
- Sugars - 16.7 g
- Protein - 68 g

Ingredients

- 1 lb. chicken thighs or breast, boneless, skinless
- 2 tbsp. olive oil
- ½ cup low-sodium chicken broth
- ½ tsp salt
- 1 dash of black pepper
- ½ tsp tarragon
- 2 tbsp. red onion, cut into wedges
- 1 red bell pepper, sliced
- 1 clove of garlic, minced
- 1 bay leaf, ground or crushed
- 1/3 cup prunes, pitted and sliced
- 1/3 cup dried apricots, sliced
- 2 tbsp. fresh parsley or other greens, for garnish

Steps/Directions:

1. Preheat the oven to 400°F. Cut chicken into small chunks.
2. Pour some oil into a skillet, add chicken, and season with salt, black pepper, tarragon, and bay leaves. Cook on medium heat for 5 mins per side.
3. Add onions, bell pepper, and garlic and continue to cook for another 3 mins.
4. Add chicken broth, prunes, and dried apricots, cover the skillet with a lid, and cook for another 7-10 mins until the chicken is fully cooked.
5. Garnish with fresh parsley and serve.

Chicken Zoodles

Prep: 5 min
Cook Time: 10 min
Total time: 15 min
Servings: 2

> One zucchini has just 25 calories! Including this vegetable in your meals may improve digestion, lower blood sugar levels, improve eye health, boost energy, help with weight loss, improve thyroid and adrenal functions, and protect against oxidation and inflammation.

Ingredients

- 2 chicken breasts, skinless and boneless, cut into pieces
- 2 tbsp. olive oil
- 2 tbsp. onions, chopped
- 3 cloves garlic, minced
- 3 zucchini, spiralized
- 1/2 tsp salt
- 1/4 tsp turmeric (optional)
- 1 dash black pepper
- 1 tbsp. lemon juice

Steps/Directions:

1. Preheat a skillet, pour some olive oil and cook onions for 3-4 mins. Add garlic and cook for one more min.
2. Add chicken. Season with salt, black pepper, and turmeric, and cook for 8-10 mins or until cooked through.
3. Add spiralized zucchini, season with lemon juice, and cook for another 1-2 mins.

Nutrition Facts Amount Per Serving

- Calories - 365.1
- Total Fat - 18.7 g
- Saturated Fat - 2.9 g
- Cholesterol - 130.0 mg
- Sodium - 726 mg
- Potassium - 820 mg
- Total Carbohydrate - 12.6 g
- Dietary Fiber - 3.6 g
- Sugars - 5.6 g
- Protein - 43 g

Chili Lime Chicken Drumsticks

Prep: 15 min
Cook Time: 45 min
Total time: 60 min
Servings: 2

> *Despite the heat, cayenne has a reasonably mild aroma. Use this spice in small amounts while cooking, so it doesn't overtake a dish.*

Nutrition Facts Amount Per Serving

- Calories - 360
- Total Fat - 18.8 g
- Saturated Fat - 9.0 g
- Cholesterol - 185.1 mg
- Sodium - 773.4 mg
- Potassium - 130 mg
- Total Carbohydrate - 7.7 g
- Dietary Fiber - 1.8 g
- Sugars - 0.8 g
- Protein - 31 g

Ingredients

- 4 medium chicken drumsticks, skinless
- ½ tsp salt
- ½ tsp black pepper
- 1 lime, sliced (for garnish)
- For marinade:
- 2 tbsp. unsalted butter, melted
- 1 tsp chili powder
- 1 tsp smoked paprika
- 1 tbsp. lime juice
- 1 clove garlic, minced
- ¼ tsp cayenne pepper

Steps/Directions:

1. Preheat your oven to 400°F. Make 2-3 cuts on each drumstick. Season the chicken with salt and black pepper.

2. In a small bowl, mix all the ingredients of the marinade. Pour the marinade into a Ziploc plastic bag and place the chicken drumsticks into it. Make sure the chicken is covered well with the marinade. You can leave the chicken in the plastic bag in the fridge for 1 hour. Or you can cook it right away.

3. Place the chicken into a baking pan and cook for 45 mins until the crispy crust. Garnish with slices of fresh lime.

Cornish Game Hens with Garlic and Rosemary

Prep: 10 min
Cook Time: 60 min
Total time: 70 min
Servings: 4

Cornish hens contain less fat and fewer calories than regular chickens. Their meat is lean. If you would like to add elegance to your dinner table, Cornish hens are a perfect choice.

Nutrition Facts Amount Per Serving

- Calories – 514
- Total Fat - 38.9 g
- Saturated Fat - 14.4 g
- Cholesterol – 249 mg
- Sodium – 2,082.7 mg
- Potassium – 1,323.0 mg
- Total Carbohydrate -18.39 g
- Dietary Fiber - 6.1 g
- Sugars - 7.7 g
- Protein - 50.5 g

Ingredients

- 4 Cornish Game Hens
- 4 tablespoons unsalted butter, melted
- 4 lemon wedges
- 6 scallions, cut
- 1 tablespoon olive oil
- 1 tablespoon lemon juice
- 2 garlic cloves, minced
- 4 carrots, sliced
- 4 celery stalks, cut
- 5 springs of rosemary
- salt and black pepper to your taste
- 2 teaspoons smoked paprika (optional)
- 2 teaspoons Italian herbs seasoning
- 1 tbsp. dried cranberries (optional)
- sage leaves (optional)

Steps/Directions:

1. Preheat the oven to 400° F. Grease a roasting pan with olive oil.
2. Place the scallions and lemon wedges inside of the hens, and tie the legs together. Season the hens with salt, black pepper, and Italian herbs seasoning, and put them in the roasting pan.
3. In a bowl, combine melted butter, lemon juice, garlic, and paprika. Pour half of the mixture over the hens. Bake for 30 mins.
4. Add carrots, celery, and rosemary to the roasting pan between the hens, and sprinkle the rest of the butter mixture and cranberries on top of the hens. Continue to bake for another 30 mins.
5. Place the hens on serving plates. Arrange the vegetables on the side of each plate and garnish them with sage leaves.

Creamy Baked Chicken

Prep: 10 min
Cook Time: 20 min
Total time: 30 min
Servings: 4

Using lime peel and lime juice in your recipes may slow the buildup of plaque on artery walls.
Limes are stronger in flavor than lemons, so generally, a smaller amount is enough to add a tropical note to your dish.

Nutrition Facts Amount Per Serving

- Calories – 492
- Total Fat - 22.1 g
- Saturated Fat - 7.2 g
- Cholesterol – 202 mg
- Sodium - 568.3 mg
- Potassium - 585 mg
- Total Carbohydrate - 3.4 g
- Dietary Fiber - 0.3 g
- Sugars - 0.6 g
- Protein – 67 g

Ingredients

- 4 chicken breasts or thighs, boneless and skinless
- 2 tbsp. olive oil
- 2 tbsp. onion, chopped
- 2 cloves garlic, minced
- 1 cup of water
- 2 tbsp. lime juice
- 2 tbsp. cilantro, chopped
- salt, and black pepper to taste
- 1/4 tsp turmeric
- 1/2 cup heavy cream or sour cream

Steps/Directions:

1. Preheat the oven to 400°F.
2. Season the chicken with salt and pepper. Heat some oil in a skillet and add the chicken. Cook for 2-3 mins per side. Then move the chicken to a baking pan.
3. In the same skillet, add onion, cook it for 2-3 mins, then add garlic and cook for another one min. Add water, lime juice, heavy cream, and cilantro. Season the sauce with salt and pepper. Mix the sauce well and pour it over the chicken. Bake for 20 mins.
4. Garnish with fresh cilantro and serve.

Zucchini Chicken Rolls

Prep: 10 min
Cook Time: 15 min
Total time: 25 min
Servings: 4

Crushed garlic cloves release enzymes that trigger the creation of sulfur compounds that are responsible for the pungent and long-lasting odor of garlic. You should store garlic unpeeled in a dark, cool, dry place. Drinking lemon juice or eating a few slices of lemon will stop bad garlic breath.

Nutrition Facts Amount Per Serving

- Calories – 882
- Total Fat - 54 g
- Saturated Fat - 16.8 g
- Cholesterol – 318 mg
- Sodium -2609 mg
- Potassium - 510 mg
- Total Carbohydrate - 12 g
- Dietary Fiber - 2.7 g
- Sugars - 5.6 g
- Protein – 83 g

Ingredients

- 3 zucchinis, peeled into long strips
- 2 cups shredded rotisserie chicken
- 2 tbsp. onions, diced
- 2 cloves garlic, minced
- ½ tsp salt
- black pepper to taste
- ½ tsp paprika
- ½ lime, juiced
- ½ cup marinara sauce
- 2 cups shredded mozzarella
- 2 tbsp. olive oil
- grated Parmesan cheese, for serving
- fresh greens, chopped for garnish

Steps/Directions:

1. Preheat the oven to 400°F. In a large bowl, mix shredded chicken with onion, garlic, salt, black pepper, paprika, lime juice, marinara sauce, and mozzarella cheese.
2. Peel long slices of zucchini and season them with salt.
3. Scoop some chicken mixture and spread it on a slice of zucchini, then roll it and fix it with a wooden toothpick.
4. Grease a baking pan with olive oil, place the zucchini rolls, and bake for 15 mins.
5. Sprinkle with Parmesan cheese, garnish with fresh greens, and serve.

Rotisserie Chicken Spinach Casserole

Prep: 10 min
Cook Time: 60 min
Total time: 70 min
Servings: 4

Store onions in a cool, dark area.

It is not recommended to keep onions in the fridge. The onion smell can spoil the flavor of other groceries in your fridge.

Nutrition Facts Amount Per Serving

- Calories – 1190
- Total Fat - 78 g
- Saturated Fat - 27.4 g
- Cholesterol – 598 mg
- Sodium - 3410 mg
- Potassium - 747 mg
- Total Carbohydrate - 12 g
- Dietary Fiber - 1.9 g
- Sugars - 7.4 g
- Protein – 108 g

Ingredients

- 2 ½ cups rotisserie chicken meat, chopped
- 2 tbsp. olive oil
- 1 cup frozen spinach
- 4 large eggs
- 1 cup farmer cottage cheese
- 1 cup Mozzarella cheese, shredded
- 1 cup sour cream
- 3 tbsp. onions, chopped
- 2 cloves garlic, minced
- 1 tsp Italian Herbs Seasoning
- ½ tsp salt
- 1 dash of black pepper
- 2 tbsp. fresh parsley or basil, chopped

Steps/Directions:

1. Preheat the oven to 400°F.
2. Preheat a large skillet, add frozen spinach, and cook for 2-3 mins. Pour olive oil, and add onions. Cook for 2 mins until fragrant and add garlic. Cook for one more min and turn off the heat. Add rotisserie chicken and mix to combine.
3. Replace everything in a baking pan, spread evenly, and top with Mozzarella cheese.
4. In a bowl, mix eggs, cottage cheese, sour cream, Italian Herbs Seasoning, salt, and black pepper.
5. Pour the mixture into the baking pan.
6. Bake for 50-60 mins.
7. Garnish with fresh greens, and let the casserole cool down for 5-10 mins before serving.

Crispy Spicy Chicken Wings

Prep: 10 min
Cook Time: 40 min
Total time: 50 min
Servings: 2

Apple cider vinegar is an ideal ingredient for any marinade for a meat dish. As a powerful bactericide, it helps eliminate any impurities.

Ingredients

- 1,5-2 lb. chicken wings
- ½ tsp salt
- 1 dash black pepper
- 2 tbsp. unsalted butter, melted
- 2 tsp baking powder
- 2 cloves garlic, minced
- 1 tbsp. smoked paprika
- 1 tbsp. apple cider vinegar

Steps/Directions:

1. Preheat the oven to 400 °F. Season chicken wings with salt and black pepper.
2. In a bowl, mix butter, baking powder, garlic, paprika, and apple cider vinegar. Coat the chicken wings with the sauce.
3. Place the chicken wings on a lined baking sheet and bake for 35-40 mins.

Nutrition Facts Amount Per Serving

- Calories – 983
- Total Fat - 45.1 g
- Saturated Fat - 16.3 g
- Cholesterol - 434 mg
- Sodium – 983 mg
- Potassium - 1706 mg
- Total Carbohydrate - 6.4 g
- Dietary Fiber - 1.4 g
- Sugars - 1.4 g
- Protein - 133 g

Garlic Parmesan Chicken Wings

Prep: 5 min
Cook Time: 40 min
Total time: 45 min
Servings: 4

When baking powder, not to be mistaken with baking soda, is mixed with salt and coated on chicken, it dries out the skin, leaving it crisp and crunchy.

Nutrition Facts Amount Per Serving

- Calories – 637
- Total Fat - 35.6 g
- Saturated Fat - 13.3 g
- Cholesterol - 237 mg
- Sodium - 790 mg
- Potassium - 817 mg
- Total Carbohydrate - 2.8 g
- Dietary Fiber - 0.2 g
- Sugars - 0 g
- Protein - 75 g

Ingredients

- 2 lb. chicken wings
- 2 tbsp. olive oil
- ½ tsp salt
- 1 dash black pepper
- 2 tsp baking powder
- 2 cloves garlic, minced
- 1 tsp Italian Herbs Seasoning
- 2 tbsp. unsalted butter, melted
- 1/2 cup Parmesan cheese, grated
- 2 tbsp. fresh greens, for garnish

Steps/Directions:

1. Preheat the oven to 400°F.
2. In a big bowl, coat chicken wings with the baking powder and season with salt, black pepper, and Italian Herbs Seasoning.
3. Place the chicken wings on a lined baking sheet and sprinkle with olive oil. Bake for 35-40 mins until crispy.
4. In a bowl, mix melted butter with Parmesan cheese, garlic, and fresh greens. Replace the chicken wings in the bowl with the mixture and toss well to coat.

Italian Chicken Breasts

Prep: 10 min
Cook Time: 25 min
Total time: 35 min
Servings: 2

> Besides its aroma, basil has high nutritional value. This herb is a rich source of vitamins A, B6, C, and K and minerals such as iron, manganese, and magnesium. The fresh leaves are primarily used, but you may use the flower buds for garnish or in a salad.

Nutrition Facts Amount Per Serving

- Calories – 819
- Total Fat - 44.7 g
- Saturated Fat - 16.5 g
- Cholesterol - 265 mg
- Sodium - 1659 mg
- Potassium - 1158 mg
- Total Carbohydrate -12.3 g
- Dietary Fiber - 2.6 g
- Sugars - 6.1 g
- Protein – 90 g

Ingredients

- 1 lb. boneless skinless chicken breasts
- 1 tbsp. olive oil
- ½ tsp. salt
- 1 dash black pepper
- ¼ cup lemon juice
- 2 cloves garlic, minced
- 1 pt. grape tomatoes halved
- 2 tbsp. fresh basil
- 4 slices Mozzarella cheese
- 4 slices Salami
- ½ tsp – turmeric, ground
- 2 tbsp. – your favorite greens for garnish (fresh parsley, dill, or green onions), chopped

Steps/Directions:

1. Preheat a frying pan and pour olive oil. Season chicken breasts with salt and pepper. Cook for 6-7 mins on each side. Put chicken aside on a plate.
2. In the same pan, cook garlic with the rest of the oil and lemon juice for about 1 min until fragrant. Add tomatoes, season them with salt, and simmer for 5-7 mins. Add basil.
3. Return chicken to the pan with tomatoes-basil sauce and put a slice of salami on each chicken breast and mozzarella cheese on top. Cover the pan with a lid until the cheese melts.
4. Sprinkle with your favorite greens and serve.

Jalapeno Pepper Chicken Casserole

Prep: 15 min
Cook Time: 40 min
Total time: 55 min
Servings: 4

Hot Mexican chili powder is hotter than regular chili powder.

Red chili powder contains a compound called capsaicin that increases the body's metabolism rate and burns fat.

Nutrition Facts Amount Per Serving

- Calories – 677
- Total Fat - 50.9 g
- Saturated Fat - 22.9 g
- Cholesterol – 274 mg
- Sodium – 1633 mg
- Potassium - 870 mg
- Total Carbohydrate - 8.0 g
- Dietary Fiber - 1.4 g
- Sugars - 3.5 g
- Protein - 50.9 g

Ingredients

- 2 lb. chicken thighs; cut to bite pieces
- 2 cups bell peppers, diced
- 3-4 jalapeno peppers, cut into stripes
- 6 oz. cream cheese
- ½ cup heavy cream or half-and-half
- 1 cup Mexican Blend Cheddar Shredded cheese
- ½ tsp – Mexican red chili powder
- 1 clove garlic, minced
- 1 tsp salt
- 4 slices bacon, cooked and crumbled
- 2 tbsp. scallions, chopped

Steps/Directions:

1. Preheat the oven to 400°F. Grease a roasting pan.
2. Place the chicken in the roasting pan. Season with salt and red chili powder.
3. Add bell peppers to the pan and mix with the chicken.
4. In a bowl, whisk heavy cream or half-and-half, cream cheese, and garlic. Pour the mixture into the roasting pan evenly.
5. Place the jalapeno peppers' stripes on top and sprinkle everything with Mexican Blend Cheddar Shredded cheese. Cover the roasting pan with aluminum foil.
6. Bake for 40 mins until the chicken is fully cooked.
7. Uncover the roasting pan, sprinkle with the bacon crumbs, and bake for 5 mins longer until golden crust.
8. Garnish with scallions and serve.

Parmesan Chicken Drumsticks

Prep: 10 min
Cook Time: 45 min
Total time: 55 min
Servings: 2

Although turmeric is traditionally found in Indian curries, this spice features in a variety of American dishes and condiments. Turmeric is used to color American processed cheese, mustard, butter, yellow cake mix, popcorn, and many other products.

Ingredients

- 4 medium chicken drumsticks
- 2 tbsp. olive oil or olive oil spray
- 1/3 cup Parmesan cheese, grated
- 1 clove garlic, minced
- 2 tbsp. onions, finely chopped
- 1 tsp Italian herbs seasoning
- ½ tsp turmeric powder
- ½ tsp salt
- ½ tsp black pepper

Steps/Directions:

1. Preheat your oven to 400°F.
2. In a small bowl, mix Parmesan cheese, garlic, onions, Italian herbs seasoning, turmeric powder, salt, and black pepper.
3. Coat each drumstick in the cheese-seasonings mixture and put it in a baking pan. Sprinkle or spray the drumsticks with olive oil.
4. Bake for 45 mins until the crispy crust. Serve with grilled vegetables.

Nutrition Facts Amount Per Serving

- Calories – 420
- Total Fat - 28.3 g
- Saturated Fat - 9.4 g
- Cholesterol - 111 mg
- Sodium - 1047 mg
- Potassium - 224 mg
- Total Carbohydrate - 3.6 g
- Dietary Fiber - 0.5 g
- Sugars - 0.5 g
- Protein - 39.1 g

Pesto Chicken Casserole

Prep: 10 min
Cook Time: 20 min
Total time: 30 min
Servings: 4

Black pepper discourages intestinal gas from forming and helps in the breakdown of fat cells. Pepper loses flavor and aroma through evaporation. Airtight storage helps preserve its spiciness longer. Pepper can also lose flavor when exposed to light.

Nutrition Facts Amount Per Serving

- Calories – 631
- Total Fat - 41.9 g
- Saturated Fat - 19.9 g
- Cholesterol – 239 mg
- Sodium – 1052 mg
- Potassium - 571 mg
- Total Carbohydrate - 6.0 g
- Dietary Fiber - 1.4 g
- Sugars - 2.8 g
- Protein - 55.8 g

Ingredients

- 1.5 lb. chicken thighs, boneless, skinless
- 1/3 cup green pesto sauce, low-carb
- 2 tbsps. butter, unsalted
- ½ tsp. salt
- 1 dash black pepper
- 1 cup heavy whipping cream
- 2/3 cup pitted olives
- 1 big tomato, sliced
- 5 oz. feta cheese, diced
- 1 garlic clove, minced

Steps/Directions:

1. Preheat your oven to 400°F.
2. Cut the chicken into small cubes and season it with salt and black pepper.
3. Add butter to a large skillet and fry chicken pieces until golden brown, 5-6 mins.
4. In a bowl, mix pesto sauce and heavy whipping cream.
5. Replace the chicken into a baking pan, add olives, feta cheese, tomatoes, and garlic on top, and pour the pesto-cream mixture.
6. Bake for 20-30 mins until light brown.

Pesto Parmesan Chicken

Prep: 10 min
Cook Time: 25 min
Total time: 35 min
Servings: 4

> Basil pesto is a good source of iron and vitamins A and C, but its' sodium content can be very high.
>
> The health benefits of basil include supporting a healthy brain, managing stress, and aid metabolism.

Nutrition Facts Amount Per Serving

- Calories - 337
- Total Fat - 16.1 g
- Saturated Fat - 6.3 g
- Cholesterol - 149 mg
- Sodium - 486 mg
- Potassium - 386 mg
- Total Carbohydrate - 2.0 g
- Dietary Fiber - 0.8 g
- Sugars - 0.9 g
- Protein - 45 g

Ingredients

- 4 chicken thighs
- 3 oz. sliced Bella mushrooms
- 1 clove garlic, minced
- 1/3 cup basil pesto
- 1/3 cup water
- 1/3 cup heavy cream
- 2 tbsp. Parmesan cheese, grated
- ½ tsp. salt
- 1 dash black pepper
- 2 tbsp. fresh leaves parsley or basil for garnish

Steps/Directions:

1. Season chicken with salt and black pepper. Preheat a skillet, add some oil and cook chicken over medium heat for 5-8 mins per side. Then put the chicken aside.
2. Use the same skillet; add more oil if needed. Then add mushrooms, season with salt and cook for 5-6 mins. Add garlic and sauté for 1 min until fragrant.
3. Add pesto and mix well. Then add water and heavy cream, and mix to combine. Sauté for 1-2 min.
4. Stir in Parmesan cheese (leave a little bit for topping) and continue to cook the sauce until cheese is melted (for about 2 mins).
5. Return chicken to the skillet and coat well with the sauce. Sprinkle with the rest of the Parmesan and garnish with fresh parsley or basil.

Rotisserie Chicken and Salad Lunch Bowl

Prep: 15 min
Total time: 15 min
Servings: 4

A small red onion will meet 10% of the daily need for vitamin C. Just like other red fruits and vegetables, red onions contain plenty of antioxidants.

Ingredients

- 1 rotisserie chicken
- 1 large cucumber, sliced
- 3 oz. grape tomatoes; cut into halves
- ¼ red onion, sliced into wedges
- 1 avocado, peeled, pitted and diced
- lettuce leaves, chopped
- 2 tbsp. walnuts, chopped
- 2 tbsp. cilantro, chopped
- 2 tbsp. olive oil
- 2 tbsp. lemon juice
- salt and black pepper to taste

Steps/Directions:

1. Cut the chicken into pieces, remove the bones and slice the meat.
2. Mix together lettuce, cucumber, grape tomatoes, onion, avocado, walnuts, and cilantro and add to the chicken.
3. Dress the salad with olive oil and lemon juice, and season it with salt and pepper.

Nutrition Facts Amount Per Serving

- Calories – 496
- Total Fat - 33.3 g
- Saturated Fat - 7.3 g
- Cholesterol – 175 mg
- Sodium - 718 mg
- Potassium – 438 mg
- Total Carbohydrate - 13.1g
- Dietary Fiber - 4.4 g
- Sugars - 3.6 g
- Protein - 41.3 g

Sheet Pan Chicken Sausage and Vegetables

Prep: 10 min
Cook Time: 20 min
Total time: 30 min
Servings: 2

Lemons may change and enhance the flavor of any dish as salt. Lemon juice changes a food's texture, as when macerating berries, tenderizing meat, and "cooking" ceviche. Lemon juice contains citric acid, which helps break down fats, carbohydrates, and protein.

Nutrition Facts Amount Per Serving

- Calories - 277.7
- Total Fat - 19.8 g
- Saturated Fat - 3.7 g
- Cholesterol – 37 mg
- Sodium – 1638 mg
- Potassium - 334 mg
- Total Carbohydrate - 13.6 g
- Dietary Fiber - 4.6 g
- Sugars - 6 g
- Protein - 15.2 g

Ingredients

- 1 lb. Italian chicken sausage, sweet, mild, or spicy
- 2 tbsp. extra-virgin olive oil
- 1 tsp Italian herbs seasoning
- 1 tsp salt
- 1 dash black pepper
- 1 tbsp. lemon juice
- 2 cups broccoli florets
- 2 bell peppers, your preferred colors, sliced
- 5 oz. grape tomatoes; cut in halves
- 2 cloves garlic, minced

Steps/Directions:

1. Preheat the oven to 400°F. Drizzle a baking sheet with olive oil.
2. Cook the sausage in boiling water for 15 mins. Let it cool down and cut it into round pieces.
3. Place the pieces of sausage and vegetables on a baking sheet.
4. Whisk olive oil, salt, black pepper, Italian herbs seasoning, lemon juice, and garlic and drizzle the mixture on the sausage and vegetables.
5. Bake for 10 -12 mins until the vegetables are soft and the sausage is fully cooked.

Sheet Pan Chicken with Green Vegetables

Prep: 15 min
Cook Time: 40 min
Total time: 55 min
Servings: 4

> *Lemon zest is exceptionally flavorful and adds so much freshness to your favorite dishes. Unlike the juice of lemons, the zest contains essential oils, more flavor, and is not as acidic or tart. When zesting lemons, limes, or oranges, you want to make sure to remove only the brightly colored flesh of the peel. Avoid the white part directly underneath the peel, as this is quite bitter.*

Nutrition Facts Amount Per Serving

- Calories – 623
- Total Fat - 44.7 g
- Saturated Fat - 11.6 g
- Cholesterol - 190 mg
- Sodium - 771 mg
- Potassium - 292 mg
- Total Carbohydrate - 9.9 g
- Dietary Fiber - 3.6 g
- Sugars - 3.3 g
- Protein - 43.9 g

Ingredients

- 4 bone-in chicken thighs
- 2 tbsp. extra-virgin olive oil
- 1 tsp salt, divided
- 1 dash black pepper
- 1 tbsp. sesame oil
- 1 tbsp. lemon juice
- 1 tsp lemon zest
- 1 medium lemon, sliced
- 1 tsp Italian herbs seasoning
- 1 cup frozen broccoli florets
- 1 cup frozen green peas
- 1 bunch of asparagus, hard ends removed
- 2 cloves garlic, minced

Steps/Directions:

1. Preheat the oven to 400°F. Drizzle a baking sheet with olive oil.

2. Season chicken with ½ tsp salt, and black pepper, toss it well and place it on the baking sheet.

3. Whisk together sesame oil, garlic, Italian herbs seasoning, lemon juice, and lemon zest, and drizzle half of this mixture on top of the chicken. Place the lemon slices on the chicken, cover everything with foil, and bake for 30 mins.

4. Uncover the chicken, and add broccoli florets, green peas, and asparagus on the baking sheet around the chicken. Pour the remaining seasoning mixture on the vegetables and continue to bake for another 10 mins uncovered until the chicken is fully cooked and the vegetables are soft and tender.

Spicy Chicken Drumsticks

Prep: 10 min
Cook Time: 45 min
Total time: 55 min
Servings: 2

Cayenne pepper powder will last longer than fresh cayenne peppers, and because it is dried, the spiciness is more concentrated.

Nutrition Facts Amount Per Serving

- Calories - 426.42
- Total Fat - 34.2 g
- Saturated Fat - 7.2 g
- Cholesterol - 104.9 mg
- Sodium - 660.4 mg
- Potassium - 280.4 mg
- Total Carbohydrate - 3.3 g
- Dietary Fiber - 1.4 g
- Sugars – 0.4 g
- Protein - 26.2 g

Ingredients

- 4 medium chicken drumsticks, skinless

For marinate

- 4 tbsp. olive oil
- 1 tbsp. heavy cream or sour cream
- 1 tsp mustard, your favorite brand
- ½ tsp turmeric powder (optional)
- ¼ tsp cayenne pepper, ground
- 1 tsp Italian herbs seasoning
- 1 clove garlic, minced
- 2 tsp paprika
- ½ tsp salt
- ½ tsp black pepper

Steps/Directions:

1. Preheat your oven to 400°F. Make 2-3 cuts on each drumstick.

2. In a small bowl, mix all the ingredients of the marinade. Pour the marinade into a Ziploc plastic bag and place the chicken drumsticks into it. Make sure the chicken is covered well with the marinade. You can leave the chicken in the plastic bag in the fridge for 1 hour. Or you can cook it right away.

3. Place the chicken into a pan and bake for 45 mins until the crispy crust.

Teriyaki Chicken Drumsticks

Prep: 10 min
Cook Time: 45 min
Total time: 55 min
Servings: 2

Ginger works well with other spices, like coriander and cumin, garlic, turmeric, and mustard in savory dishes, and cinnamon and cloves in sweet recipes.

Nutrition Facts Amount Per Serving

- Calories - 330.02
- Total Fat - 20.0 g
- Saturated Fat - 3.7 g
- Cholesterol – 81 mg
- Sodium - 919 mg
- Potassium - 394.5 mg
- Total Carbohydrate - 6.6 g
- Dietary Fiber - 0.8 g
- Sugars – 4.1 g
- Protein - 28.1 g

Ingredients

- 4 medium chicken drumsticks
- 2 tbsp. olive oil
- ½ tsp salt
- ½ tsp black pepper
- ¼ cup soy low-sodium sauce
- 2 packages Stevia
- 1 clove garlic, minced
- 1 tsp ginger, powder or grated
- 1 tsp apple cider vinegar
- molasses, few drops for color (optional)
- 1 tbsp. sesame seeds

Steps/Directions:

1. Preheat your oven to 400°F. Place the chicken drumsticks in a baking pan. Season chicken with salt and black pepper and sprinkle with olive oil.
2. In a small bowl, mix soy sauce, apple cider vinegar, molasses, Stevia, garlic, and ginger. Pour the mixture on top of the chicken. Sprinkle with sesame seeds.
3. Bake for 45 mins until the crispy crust.

Tex Mex Chicken Salad

Prep: 10 min
Cook Time: 20 min
Total time: 30 min
Servings: 4

> Cumin seeds in Indian cuisine are often chewed as a digestive aid and may be offered at Indian restaurants after a meal for this purpose. Because the flavor of ground cumin is more concentrated than whole cumin seeds, you need it less in a dish. For a recipe that calls for 1 tablespoon of ground cumin, use 1 1/4 tablespoons of cumin seeds.

Nutrition Facts Amount Per Serving

- Calories - 454
- Total Fat – 17.5 g
- Saturated Fat - 4.7 g
- Cholesterol - 202 mg
- Sodium - 1275 mg
- Potassium - 620 mg
- Total Carbohydrate - 3.7 g
- Dietary Fiber - 0.4 g
- Sugars - 1.1 g
- Protein - 67 g

Ingredients

- 2 boneless skinless chicken breasts
- 2 tbsp. extra-virgin olive oil
- 2 bell peppers, sliced into stripes
- 2 tbsp. red onion, cut into wedges
- 1 clove garlic, minced
- 6 lettuce leaves
- avocado, sliced
- 2 Roma tomatoes, diced
- 1 cucumber, diced
- 1 tbsp. feta cheese
- 2 tbsp. cilantro, chopped
- ½ tsp paprika
- 1 tsp cumin
- ½ tsp ground mustard
- juice of ½ lime
- few almond nuts, optional
- salt and black pepper to taste

Steps/Directions:

1. Mix salt, black pepper, mustard, paprika, and cumin. Divide into two parts.
2. Preheat a skillet and add some olive oil. Add onions and garlic, and cook for 2-3 mins. Add bell peppers, season with one-half of the spices, and cook for another 3-4 mins. Replace everything on a plate.
3. Add some olive oil to the same skillet and add chicken breasts. Season with the remaining spices. Cook for 5-6 mins on each side or until the chicken is cooked through. Let it cool down and cut it into slices or bite pieces.
4. Arrange the lettuce leaves on a serving plate and put chicken and bell peppers on top.
5. Add avocado, tomatoes, cucumber, cilantro, feta cheese, and nuts. Sprinkle everything with lime juice.

Zucchini and Ground Chicken Boats

Prep: 10 min
Cook Time: 20 min
Total time: 30 min
Servings: 4

When you cook meat with vegetables, coat each piece in a mixture of olive oil, cinnamon, cumin, fresh garlic, and salt before roasting.

Nutrition Facts Amount Per Serving

- Calories - 232.2
- Total Fat - 11.7 g
- Saturated Fat - 4.2 g
- Cholesterol – 63 mg
- Sodium - 509 mg
- Potassium - 498 mg
- Total Carbohydrate - 6.6 g
- Dietary Fiber - 1.8 g
- Sugars - 2.9 g
- Protein - 24.4 g

Ingredients

- 8 ounces ground chicken
- 2 medium zucchini
- 2 tbsp. onion, chopped
- 1 clove garlic, minced
- ½ tsp cinnamon
- 2 tbsp. tomato paste
- 1 tsp Italian herbs seasoning
- 2 tbsp. fresh parsley, chopped
- 1 tbsp. olive oil
- 2 tbsp. grated Parmesan cheese
- 2 tbsp. Mozzarella cheese, grated
- ½ tsp salt
- 1 dash black pepper
- 1 tbsp. fresh parsley or other greens for garnish

Steps/Directions:

1. Cut each zucchini in halves lengthwise and clean out the middle. Now you have 4 "zucchini boats." Place in a baking dish with a lid and cook in the microwave on high for 4 minutes or bake in the oven at 375°F for 10-12 minutes or until cooked through.
2. In a sauté pan, add olive oil and cook onions and garlic until beginning to turn translucent. Add ground chicken, season it with salt, black pepper, Italian herbs, and cinnamon, and cook until browned.
3. Add tomato paste, Parmesan cheese, and parsley. Cook for another 2 minutes.
4. Divide the stuffing between the zucchini boats. Sprinkle with Mozzarella cheese, garnish with parsley, and serve.

Zucchini Chicken Lasagna

Prep: 25 min
Cook Time: 20 min
Total time: 45 min
Servings: 6

> Sprinkle zucchini with salt and let it sit for 10 minutes. Salt will draw excess moisture out of the zucchini, preventing the lasagna from being runny and liquidy.

Nutrition Facts Amount Per Serving

- Calories – 505
- Total Fat - 32.4 g
- Saturated Fat - 15.7 g
- Cholesterol – 168 mg
- Sodium - 553.9 mg
- Potassium - 707 mg
- Total Carbohydrate - 7.4 g
- Dietary Fiber - 1.9 g
- Sugars - 3.4 g
- Protein – 45 g

Ingredients

- 3 zucchini, finely sliced
- 2 tbsp. olive oil
- 2 tbsp. onions, chopped
- 2 garlic cloves, minced
- 1.5 lb. ground chicken
- 1 tbsp. Italian herbs seasoning
- ½ tsp salt
- 1 dash black pepper
- 1 tsp cinnamon
- 4 tbsp. tomato paste
- 1 cup heavy whipping cream
- 2 cups cheese, shredded
- 2 tbsp. fresh greens, for garnish

Steps/Directions:

1. Preheat your oven to 400°F.
2. Slice the zucchini thinly; season the slices with salt.
3. Heat the oil in a skillet and add onions, sauté for 2 mins, add 1 garlic clove and cook for another 1 min. Then add the ground chicken, Italian herbs, cinnamon, salt, and black pepper to taste. Cook for 5-6 mins.
4. Stir in tomato paste and simmer for another 2 mins.
5. In a saucepan, mix together the heavy whipping cream and half of the shredded cheese, 1 garlic clove. Bring to boiling, reduce the heat, and simmer for 5 mins stirring continuously until the sauce is thickened.
6. Assemble the lasagna: spread 1/3 of the meat sauce on the bottom of the baking pan, pour some cheese sauce on top, and cover with zucchini slices in one layer. Repeat the layers 2-3 times. Sprinkle the last layer with the remaining cheese.
7. Bake in the oven for 18-20 mins, until the cheese is golden. Cool the lasagna down for 10-15 mins, garnish with greens, and serve.

Buffalo Chicken Wings

Prep: 10 min
Cook Time: 45 min
Total time: 55 min
Servings: 4

> *Baking powder is alkaline, so it raises the pH level of chicken skin and jumpstarts the browning process. Make sure your baking powder is aluminum-free. Use baking powder and NOT baking SODA. Using baking soda will give your wings an off-taste.*

Nutrition Facts Amount Per Serving

- Calories – 195
- Total Fat - 20.4 g
- Saturated Fat - 8.8 g
- Cholesterol – 38 mg
- Sodium - 210 mg
- Potassium - 122 mg
- Total Carbohydrate - 2.3 g
- Dietary Fiber - 0.2 g
- Sugars - 1 g
- Protein - 25.9 g

Ingredients

- 12-16 chicken wings
- ·2 tbsp. olive oil
- ·½ tsp baking powder
- ·½ tsp paprika
- ·salt and black pepper to taste

Keto Buffalo Sauce Ingredients

- 4-5 tbsps. your favorite hot sauce, low sugar
- 4 tbsp. unsalted butter
- 1 tsp blackstrap molasses
- ¼ tsp cayenne pepper (optional)
- 2 cloves garlic, minced

Steps/Directions:

1. Preheat the oven to 400°F. Place the chicken wings on a baking sheet, sprinkle with olive oil and baking powder, and season with salt and black pepper. Bake for 35 mins.
2. In a bowl, mix melted butter, hot sauce, blackstrap molasses, garlic, and cayenne pepper.
3. Pour the sauce over the chicken wings and continue to bake for another 10 mins. Serve hot and enjoy!

Best foods to eat on the keto diet

So, how much protein per day should you eat on a keto diet?

Many of us can be confused about that when someone first starts a keto diet. So, what is the optimal amount of protein for achieving the results you want from keto?

If you eat too little protein, you may lose too much muscle weight. But if you get too much protein, it may happen that your body will turn the excess protein into glucose, and that will mess up your ketosis. Your body will be burning glucose for energy instead of working on burning extra fat.

The keto experts say that we should eat 90-120 g of protein each day. You can get that if you have 1,5 chicken breasts or two 6-8 oz steaks per day.

Seafood

Fish and shellfish are on the keto groceries list. Even though they contain some amount of carbs, these foods are also rich in B vitamins, potassium, and selenium.

However, different types of shellfish vary in carbs. While shrimp and crabs have no carbs at all, oysters, and octopuses contain a certain amount of carbohydrates. You can still eat your favorite seafood products and carefully check the carbs to make sure you stay within your range.

In addition to that, salmon, sardines, mackerel, and some other fatty fish are very high in omega-3.

Meat and poultry

You can`t do a keto diet without eating meat and poultry. These foods are almost carbs-free and rich in many important minerals. It's a great source of protein.

Red meat provides our body with iron, zinc, and vitamin B complex. However, poultry meat has less cholesterol and saturated fat than most red meat.

Eggs

Eggs are ideal keto food, loaded with healthy protein.
Eggs provide our body with essential amino acids and have very few carbohydrates.
You can have only 2 eggs for breakfast and feel full and satisfied.
Egg yolk is the most nutritious part of an egg.

It is rich in iron, phosphorus, selenium, healthy cholesterol, omega-3, and vitamin D. So, it's better to use whole eggs in your recipes.

One boiled egg contains about 77 calories.

Cheese

You may choose any cheese you like and incorporate it into your keto menu. Cheese is low in carbs and is a good source of fat, animal protein, and calcium. Try to stay away from highly processed cheese. And make sure to check the nutrition facts on every package you buy. This way, you will pick the right product.

Plain Greek yogurt and cottage cheese

If you are a fan of dairy products, you may want to include plain Greek yogurt and cottage cheese into your diet. These products are good sources of protein, and they are very nutritious. Just eat them in moderation, as both of them, Greek yogurt and cottage cheese,

contain some carbs. It's always better to choose organic products made with whole milk. Add berries, chopped nuts, or pieces of fruit, and you'll have a delicious keto snack.

Cream and half-and-half

The cream is a dairy product, the higher-fat component of milk. Half-and-half is made of 50% cream and 50% whole milk. Both of these products are absolutely keto-friendly. But it's good to consume them in moderation according to the dietary guidelines of the American Heart Association. Also, if you use too many milk products in your diet, you may get too many carbs. So be careful.

Many people use whipping cream or heavy cream with coffee. It's a keto-friendly option to enjoy your favorite beverage sugar-free, but remember that any processed product contains a lot of saturated fat which is not good for your health.

Unsweetened plant-based milk

As was said before, using too much milk in your diet may compromise your ketosis. That's why it's recommended to replace regular milk with plant-based low-carb alternatives. You should choose unsweetened plant milk and always check the number of carbs.

A great option is an almond milk. It's very nutritious, good for the bones, and packed with antioxidants. Other great options are soy milk, coconut milk, pea protein milk, flax milk, and hemp milk.

At the same time, you should avoid oat milk. Even unsweetened oat milk has too many carbs.

LEAFY GREENS

Green leafy veggies are rich in vitamins, antioxidants, and minerals. And they have almost zero carbs which makes them absolutely keto-friendly.

Dark leafy greens like spinach and kale contain vitamin K and iron. Lettuce is a traditional part of many salads and is very popular in keto meals. Romaine lettuce is considered to be a healthier option.

Greens add volume to your everyday meals and help you to fill full without increasing the carb and calorie count.

Peppers

Different kinds of peppers are used in the keto diet. Hot peppers add spice to your recipes. Jalapenos are perfect for making delicious keto appetizers. You can stuff bell peppers and poblanos. Use peppers of red, yellow, orange, and green color. They will make your dishes attractive and flavorful.

Peppers are rich in vitamin C.

Summer squash

Yellow squash and zucchini are low in carbs and often used in cooking keto meals.

Start to use a spiralizer, and you can replace regular pasta with zucchini noodles. You can also grade squashes and add them to other goods. Or just slice them, toss them with olive oil, salt, and pepper, and have a cold salad.

Summer squash provides your body with a solid amount of dietary fiber that helps to keep you feeling full and can improve your digestion.

Summer squash doesn't contain cholesterol and is rich in vitamins and minerals.

High-fat veggies

Avocados and olives are very high in fat and fiber.

Olives contain antioxidants and anti-inflammatory properties. Avocados are a low-carb and high-fat food, and it's absolutely fine if you eat 1 whole avocado per day. You can add it to your salad or slice it and have it as a snack.

Both fruits are excellent sources of vitamins and minerals. And of cause, these fruits will add an extraordinary flavor to your dishes, and make your meals healthier and tastier.

Also, it's recommended to use olive oil for cooking keto dishes.

OTHER NON-STARCHY VEGETABLES

Luckily, there are quite a few vegetables low in carbs and calories but rich in nutrients. And one of them is cauliflower. You can separate its' florets and bake them. Or you can turn them into "rice" or make mashed cauliflower. You can make a few side dishes with this vegetable.

Turnips replace potatoes in keto recipes. Add this vegetable to your soups or make a separate side dish.

Other keto-friendly vegetables are asparagus, cabbage, mushrooms, broccoli, cucumbers, eggplant, green beans, tomatoes, radishes, celery, and okra.

And keep in mind that there are vegetables that you should avoid on the keto diet. They are potatoes and sweet potatoes, butternut squash, and corn. Also, beets and onions if you use them in large amounts, but you can still enjoy these vegetables in moderation.

Nuts and seeds

Nuts and seeds are great keto products, high in healthy fats and low in carbs. They are also high in fiber which helps you feel full for a longer time.

At the same time, the amount of carbs varies in different types of nuts and seeds. The best options for the keto diet are almonds, pecans, walnuts, flaxseeds, and chia seeds.

BERRIES

Among all berries, raspberries, and strawberries are the best options for the keto diet. These berries are high in fiber and low in carbs. Blackberries can be added to keto snacks and recipes as well. But blueberries have higher amounts of sugar and can`t be included in the keto groceries list.

Dark chocolate and cocoa powder

Dark chocolate is one of the most delicious sources of antioxidants. It's good for your heart as it may help lower blood pressure. Also, dark chocolate contains iron, magnesium, zinc, phosphorus, and copper. Our body needs all these elements to stay healthy.

Remember to choose dark chocolate of 70% cocoa or more and enjoy it in moderation, 1-2 squares per day.

OLIVE OIL

Extra-virgin olive oil is recommended for cooking keto recipes. It contains healthy acids and good fats; it is high in antioxidants. Olive oil has no carbs. Use it for salad dressings, and homemade mayonnaise.

Other options to try on the keto diet are coconut oil and avocado oil.

Butter and ghee

The Keto diet is about good fats and low carbs. That's why you absolutely need good quality butter and ghee (if you like this product) to prepare your meals.

Ghee is made by heating butter and removing the milk solids which makes this product carb-free. Ghee is very popular in Indian cooking.

Unsweetened coffee and tea

The good news is that coffee and tea are carb-free drinks. They both contain caffeine which helps increase your metabolism.

You may add fresh cream to your coffee or tea but stay away from highly processed creamers, they contain a lot of carbs.

You can use natural, keto-friendly sweeteners for your beverages, such as stevia, monk fruit sweetener, and yacon syrup.

There are sweeteners that you should avoid on the keto diet. They are honey, coconut sugar, maple syrup, and agave nectar.

Unsweetened sparkling water

If you are craving soda and looking for a good alternative to it, unsweetened sparkling water is a good choice. It is sugar-free and has no calories or carbs. However, some brands add fruit juice which contains carbohydrates. So always check the labels when you buy these types of drinks.

Printed in Great Britain
by Amazon

30665148R00044